JUNETEENTH STREET

Part Six
of
The City of the Bayou
Collection

Reginald Edmund

BROADWAY PLAY PUBLISHING INC
New York
www.broadwayplaypub.com
info@broadwayplaypub.com

Cover art by Reginald Edmund

First edition: December 2023
I S B N: 978-0-88145-878-7

Book design: Marie Donovan
Page make-up: Adobe InDesign
Typeface: Palatino

The City of the Bayou Collection is a series of nine plays that is a fictionalized re-imagining of the Fourth Ward of Houston. It examines what this historically Black community would look like if gentrification had never plagued it. Where one play ends, the next play begins; and where one character plays a minor role in one play, they become a major component of the next. This is the playwright's attempt at making a contemporary House of Atreus through a Afro-Surrealist lens. The nine plays, in order, are:

THE DAUGHTERS OF THE MOON

SOUTHBRIDGE

IN THE PROPHET'S HOUSE.

BLOOD ON THE BAYOU

REDEMPTION OF ALLAH BLACK

JUNETEENTH STREET

THE ORDAINED SMILE OF SADIE MAY JENKINS

THE LAST CADILLAC

ALL THE DYING VOICES

Reverend John McHenry, the protagonist of this play is the great-great grandson of Kokuma, the protagonist of THE DAUGHTERS OF THE MOON, and the great grandson of Christopher C Davis, the protagonist of SOUTHBRIDGE.

CHARACTERS & SETTING

REVEREND JOHN MCHENRY, *African American male, mid 30s*

ANGELA MCHENRY, *African American or mixed race, female, late 20s, from Chicago*

DEACON RAYMOND, *African American male, late 60s*

MAMA LOVE, *African American female, ancient*

TY SOUTHMILL, *African American male, late 20s-early 30s*

CLAIRE WINTERS, *African American female, early 30s*

The church sanctuary of Mount Saint Moses Missionary Baptist Church of the Fourth Ward.

Present day

The church is in severe need of repair. A pulpit sits on a secondary level with a piano nearby, in front of that sits an old wooden altar and an old battered wooden cross. Against the back wall stands two banners that read Mt. St. Moses Bapt. *upon them; they stand in front of two pillars with several notches carved into them, an old wooden chair sits in the center.*

Prelude

(In darkness the sound of mourning. Lights up on
REVEREND JOHN MCHENRY *stands in front of the podium.*
One hand raised high.)

*(*MAMA LOVE *an elder woman of the church, dressed in*
funeral dress sings Amazing Grace *as* MCHENRY *preaches.*
The congregation silhouetted in the darkness behind him.)

MCHENRY: Church!
I lost my father this week!
We lost our preacher this week!
This city has lost one of its greatest leaders!!!
And this community mourns…
And Church!
Even more than losing a father, a preacher, a leader to
this community!
We lost us a great lion of a man!
Yes, we should mourn today.
And yet today I'm telling you that we should rejoice.
We should rejoice because although he is gone!!!
Although he has been called away.
Although he has passed on to a better place.
Although he has entered into the Lord's house.
Greeted with open arms and the great holy father
shouting with joy "Reverend John McHenry Sr., You
done good!!! You served your people well, and now
my son Welcome on home!"
Although he is gone.

I know that he is looking down and smiling cause he knows… He knows…I said cause He knows…
That his legacy lives on!
Can the church give me an Amen!

(Audience cheering)

(Lights fade out.)

ACT ONE

Scene 1:
Fish Out of Water

(Early May in Houston)

(The scene opens on McHenry, *He walks to the pulpit and begins scribbling profusely onto a piece of paper as he prepares his Juneteenth Sermon. It's eight in the evening.)*

McHenry: How can we feed the multitude? That leads me now to my message for this evening, With only five fish, and two loaves how can we feed the multitude? *(Pause)* How can we feed the multitude? Lord, that's a damn good question.

(The sound of shattering glass interrupts McHenry.*)*

McHenry: For Christ sake—Lord help me- I can't believe they did it again—

*(An elder gentleman [*Raymond*] enters with dust pan and broom in hand.)*

Raymond: Second window they busted out this month…guess we'll have to finally break down and get us a security system.

McHenry: I wonder if Reverend Hopewell's church had to buy himself a security system… Lord, what am I doing here?

RAYMOND: Don't know what to tell you on that. We all got our flock to minister. This is yours…

MCHENRY: If you say so…what are you doing here so late anyway?

RAYMOND: I could ask you the same, boy.

MCHENRY: Doesn't answer my question.

RAYMOND: I find peace in this church…Sit here and I can almost feel your father's presence within these walls still.

MCHENRY: What time is it anyway?

RAYMOND: You got a watch don't ya?

MCHENRY: Christ… Eight.

RAYMOND: Blessed are the meek, Lord. Blessed are the meek.

MCHENRY: She's gonna kill me.

(ANGELA *enters a bottle of wine in hand. She looks at* MCHENRY *and* RAYMOND *before she interrupts.*)

ANGELA: You know someone broke your window?

MCHENRY: Thank you, I didn't notice.

ANGELA: Is that what I got to do to get your attention?

MCHENRY: Well you got it, now.

RAYMOND: How you doing, Ma'am?

ANGELA: I'm doing just fine, Deacon. My momma use to tell me if I wanted to get a good man, I needed to go to the Church. Was wondering if you knew if there were any available that might catch my interest?

RAYMOND: Well, Miss Angela, if I was a few decades younger I'd put in my bid; but I happen to know a young neighborhood preacher that's been catching the ladies interest lately. Just a hunch but I think that you might catch a liking to him. Don't know if you heard of him, handsome fellow, named John McHenry. Well, I'll let you cast your net in his direction, see if you can catch you that fish. Well, boy, I'll be in the back sweeping up glass and boardin' up that window before I call it a night. Careful Miss, that fish is slippery.

ANGELA: I think I'll manage. Talk to you later, Deacon Raymond. Hello, Reverend.

McHENRY: Ma'am.

ANGELA: Hear you supposed to be some kind of a big catch?

McHENRY: I manage alright- shame I got to tell them I've already got myself hooked on somebody's line.

ANGELA: Oh really? Well any chance this bottle of merlot will change things? 1999, according to Prince this was a good year.

McHENRY: Nice bait. What's the occasion?

ANGELA: Just finished unpacking the last of those boxes up in that big lonely house, so I figured maybe I should come over see if this merlot and maybe a few other things might open up for you—if you come home with me tonight.

McHENRY: Naughty, naughty, Miss Angela. Must I remind you that I'm a married man? A newlywed. Thank you very much…and as you can see we are in the house of the Lord.

ANGELA: Must I remind you that one half of this newlywed couple is locking himself away in a church. So, what's a girl to do but go…ummm fishing? Can't wait to see what I catch tonight. I'm kind of anxious; last one I caught was a big one. I had to mount it to the wall it was so big.

McHENRY: Angela!

ANGELA: What? I did.

MCHENRY: Thou shall not tempt thy church's Reverend when he's preparing for the big day.…

ANGELA: If you don't come home with me, I'll drink this all up without you, preacher man.

MCHENRY: Angela.

ANGELA: Do you have any idea what time it is, John? I cooked.

MCHENRY: Ordering Chinese doesn't count as 'I cooked', Angela…

ANGELA: Fine… I dialed. Come back to the house, John.

MCHENRY: My first Juneteenth sermon, baby. It has to be just right because after this sermon, I'm going to be compared forever to two generations of McHenry preachers by the congregation of Mount Saint Moses Missionary Baptist Church of Fourth Ward. *(He looks at his watch.)* Ah, Eight fourteen. Here it comes…

(A single gunshot rings out.)

ANGELA: Was that a gunshot?!

MCHENRY: Crazy, huh?

ANGELA: John, what type of neighborhood…? Gunshots!

MCHENRY: Every full moon at eight fifteen, Old Lady Goody goes out in her yard and shoots her little pistol at the moon. Grandpa use to say that she's the voodoo spirit trapped on earth or some mess like that. Use to sit me down right here after service and tell me about his wild prophecies and…God I loved his stories… Did I ever tell you the one where—

ANGELA: Not interested in stories, unless it's about Angela and her wild ride on the big fish.

You have any clue how late it is—?

MCHENRY: Angela. I'll go home, later. Just so much piled up on me. Got Mama Love talking all this mumbo jumbo about some prophecy. Calling me Moses…telling me things a man doesn't need to find out at their fathers' funeral.

ANGELA: What did she tell you?

(Silence)

MCHENRY: Silly ramblings of an old woman. Anyway, my love can you do me a favor meet? With the Women's Auxiliary group to help with Juneteenth service?

ANGELA: Marry you and become the church secretary? I gave up a career for you to come here. Don't make me regret it.

MCHENRY: Here we go!

ANGELA: For crying out loud, Last year you were one of the Top Fifty Educators of Chicago! Now look at you! This is insane.

MCHENRY: Baby, will you meet with them please?

ANGELA: We went from Chicago's Hyde Park to…to… We're living in the middle of the ghetto surrounded by crack heads and…and criminals.

MCHENRY: Were we living in the same Hyde Park?

ANGELA: I'm serious.

MCHENRY: No, you're exaggerating.

ANGELA: For Christ sake, you got some old woman shooting a damn gun at the moon. The moon, John! This is crazy! We're fish out of water here!

MCHENRY: Deacon Raymond and everybody else, thinks I don't belong here. Last thing I need is for you to join in.

ANGELA: John, you told me taking over the church was temporary…We don't belong here. Let's pack up, tell them this isn't going to work and let's go home.

MCHENRY: Angela.

ANGELA: This town is a nightmare. It's like civilization completely stopped.

MCHENRY: For Christ sake! Shit…I mean crap…damn it! Angela see what you got me doing?!! I'm a McHenry man and it's expected—

ANGELA: Oh, don't give me that tradition mess! You hate being here as much as I do.

MCHENRY: Woman!

ANGELA: Negro, don't you *dare* "woman" me! Listen, you are not your father, you are not your grandfather… you are John McHenry—

MCHENRY: Junior. John McHenry Jr., can't escape who I am.

(MCHENRY *goes behind the pulpit and pulls out a small box, reveals it to* ANGELA *and then opens it pulling out a gun from a shoebox and places it upon the altar.*)

MCHENRY: Earlier, I was thinking how ready I was to leave here and then this kid came in, had nothing to live for, nothing to believe in and I talked to him; I talked to him…this kid who was no older than fifteen…sixteen years old. He told me he witnessed his older brother shoot a man in the head, his brother's own best friend. Watched as he kneeled down after he shot him held the dying man in his arms and tried…he tried to scoop that poor man's brains off the pavement and back into his skull. The kid saw this, Angela. He told me he didn't want to leave this earth like that, and I took him by the shoulder and asked if I could pray for his soul and he pulled out this gun and put it down at the altar and we prayed. I don't know what it is- but I

felt something surge through me. You can't feel that?
Grandpa McHenry, my old man, me, our future child.
Alive. Breathing. Singing.
Preaching in that crimson robe black trim on the front.
Those sleeves outstretched wide calling for those to
come together. The walls rattling as the choir sings.
The music fills up the halls of the church. Tell me you
can feel that, Angela?

ANGELA: I can't feel a thing, preacher.

(MCHENRY *picks up the gun and puts it back into the box
and tucks it behind the sanctuary.*)

MCHENRY: It's funny but I didn't either till today. It'll
take time. Deacon Raymond, would start off church
service with that song he always sings… (*Sings*)
Bless me now, oh gentle savior
Hear my humble cry
While on…
(*Stops singing*) And here. Right here I'd stand as a child.
Just like my father did for grandpa. Carrying that
raggedy old wooden cross. Don't you see baby? I got
no choice but to be here.

ANGELA: Baby, I love you… but I think you've lost
your mind. This isn't what I want… this isn't what you
want. Is it? John, to be here?

MCHENRY: I don't… I don't honestly know…but…
look—

(MCHENRY *motions* ANGELA *to one side of the pillars in
the church. He pulls back the banner in front of one of the
pillars. Revealing several notches carved upon the pillar.*)

MCHENRY: See? Right here was me at six years old, and
then at eight and then eleven…and over here that's my
father.

(MCHENRY *guides* ANGELA *to another pillar.*)

MCHENRY: Right here him at six years, at eight and then...do you understand? I'm etched into this place forever. If I can make this work then...what would have happened to that kid if I didn't pray for him? I've decided I'm going to try to get the academy, my father dreamed of. I can help this community by opening a school. I'm needed here.

ANGELA: John?

MCHENRY: I can save this community.

(Silence)

ANGELA: You lied to me. You...you want to be here.

MCHENRY: Angela.

ANGELA: No, you said this would only be short term. We'd only stay here a few months. I can't... I can't talk to you right now. *(She moves to exit.)*

MCHENRY: Angela, look after things settle down, we'll get out of here for a little while. Go visit your mom and dad in Chicago for thanksgiving, alright how does that sound?

ANGELA: You promise?

MCHENRY: Promise, baby. Turkey, macaroni, and candy yams at your folks. Thanksgiving in the Windy City, I promise. Now can you please just make the phone calls and handle the issue with the women's auxiliary. For me...please? I'll see you when I get home.

ANGELA: Bye, John...don't be looking for the merlot when you get home. There's some homeless guy sitting on the church steps, I'll give it him. At least I know, he'll appreciate it.

MCHENRY: Angela. *(He flashes their sign that he loves her. Two pounds to his heart. Two peace signs to his chest, and then kiss it to her.)*

(ANGELA *sighs*.)

ANGELA: Love you too. (*She returns their sign for love*.)

(MCHENRY *watches as* ANGELA *leaves. He moves to the altar and gently touches it, then he touches the cross with his fingertips. The sound of* RAYMOND *singing 'Bless Me Now' is heard in the background.* MCHENRY *moves back to the speech that he's working upon*.)

MCHENRY: Brothers and sisters…the text for this Juneteenth service will be from Matthew 14, verses 14 through 18.

(*End scene*)

Scene Two:
Welcome to the Hood

(*The following day, mid afternoon*)

(MCHENRY *lies sleeping underneath the piano. Wrapped in a blanket.* RAYMOND *enters with a coffee pot and begins sweeping the floor before he notices* MCHENRY *sleeping. He moves towards him and pokes him with the broom stick handle startling him awake*.)

MCHENRY: They had two fishes. Just two… (*Notices* RAYMOND *and crawls out from under the piano*.) Oh hey, Deacon Raymond. Morning.

RAYMOND: It's afternoon, boy.

MCHENRY: Afternoon?!! Angela is gonna kill me.

RAYMOND: Next time you and your pretty Miss Angela decide to fight and she kicks you out. You sleep on your couch. I don't want you thinking this the Guzman Motel.

MCHENRY: No, no, nothing like that. Just had to finish my sermon. Closed my eyes for just a second and it was game over.

RAYMOND: Umhmph, I'm serious, boy, I'm ain't putting no mints on your pillow. You take your lover's quarrels elsewhere.

McHENRY: It's not what you think.

RAYMOND: Mrs McHenry kicked you out for the night, and you decided that you'd sleep here at the church. That's exactly what I think…you going to tell me different? Didn't think so. Why you sleeping out here anyway? You know you got an office with a couch in it right?

McHENRY: Too many memories. *(Silence)* Anyway, glad you're here. Help me with this chair.

RAYMOND: Alright.

(McHENRY with RAYMOND's help carries off the old preacher's chair and they return carrying in a new chair.)

RAYMOND: It's different.

McHENRY: What do you think?

RAYMOND: Looks fancy, where you get it?

McHENRY: Online…came earlier this morning…

RAYMOND: Was something wrong with the old chair, boy?

McHENRY: It was old.

RAYMOND: That was your father's chair… your grandfather's chair—

McHENRY: Deacon Raymond, it was old.

RAYMOND: You can't throw things out just because it doesn't suit your world. World don't work that way… That chair has been the pastor's chair ever since we were founded. What was wrong with that chair?

McHENRY: New preacher… New image for the church! And Raymond- image is everything! You're acting like I threw the old thing out. It was all worn out; no cushion, ugly to look at, so we're just put it up in the attic…you're acting like it's big deal. What are you doing here today anyway?

RAYMOND: You forgot, Brother Southmill will be here to speak with you in a few.

MCHENRY: What the hell he want?

RAYMOND: Who would have thought I'd lived to see the day this church would be under the hands of a man that curses as much as you. Listen boy, he's come here to talk about that mortgage issue. You haven't talked to him since Mama Love sat you two down at the funeral.

MCHENRY: Just tell him I'm not here. Just because Mama Love says something don't mean it's true.

RAYMOND: He's been calling over here for five days straight. Boy, you're not going to talk to the man? He deserves that at least.

MCHENRY: I'm busy.

RAYMOND: You too busy to tend to your sheep? Lord. Lord. Lord.

MCHENRY: What was that?

RAYMOND: Nothing, I'll bring him in now—

MCHENRY: Don't send him in here.

RAYMOND: Boy, from ten to two, the Reverend of this church meets with members of his congregation.

MCHENRY: Raymond, I'm not in the mood—

RAYMOND: It's not a matter of mood, boy. It's tradition… From ten to two. Congregational Care Meeting. It's twelve-twenty. From ten to—

MCHENRY: I know what time it is, Deacon. Why, wasn't I informed of this before?

RAYMOND: That's the way it has always been.

MᴄHᴇɴʀʏ: Nobody told me.

Rᴀʏᴍᴏɴᴅ: I told you.

MᴄHᴇɴʀʏ: No you didn't.

Rᴀʏᴍᴏɴᴅ: My fault. Thought I told you.

MᴄHᴇɴʀʏ: Lord help me.

Rᴀʏᴍᴏɴᴅ: Blessed are the meek. Blessed are the meek.

MᴄHᴇɴʀʏ: I can't meet with anybody right now—

Rᴀʏᴍᴏɴᴅ: As long as your father, and his father before him has lead this church. How can you not remember this?

MᴄHᴇɴʀʏ: There's a lot of things I don't remember—

Rᴀʏᴍᴏɴᴅ: Ten to two P M, boy. It's twelve-twenty-one.

MᴄHᴇɴʀʏ: From here on out I'm setting up my own meeting times. Tell him that *(we can schedule it for tomorrow)*—

Rᴀʏᴍᴏɴᴅ: Blessed are the poor, lord, blessed are the poor… Brother Southmill, come on in, preacher going to meet with you.

MᴄHᴇɴʀʏ: Thank you, Deacon Raymond.

Tʏ: John McHenry is a Reverend…welcome back home.

MᴄHᴇɴʀʏ: Thank you, it's good to be back. How can I help you, Brother Southmill?

Tʏ: Oh, so formal. Man, why you acting like you don't know me?

MᴄHᴇɴʀʏ: How are you doing Ty, long time no talk to.

Tʏ: Been like five years since you've been back home?

MᴄHᴇɴʀʏ: Something like that.

Tʏ: It's good to see you following in the family's path.

Was beginning to think you was avoiding me.

MCHENRY: How can I help you, Ty?

TY: Well, Rev, the Neighborhood Community Center is behind on payments.

MCHENRY: Like I said before I don't see how I can help?

TY: You know how it is here, we got kids walking around these streets waiting to be picked up off the corner by the cops. Not a lot of opportunities in the job market available… Lot of people are struggling here… Lot of the elderly, in this community live in our housing units. The ones that are adjacent to our center.

MCHENRY: I understand that, but the church funds are rather tight.

TY: Just asking you to realize the importance that place has. You know it's not just hope for the future of the community's soul, but it holds my soul in that place, too. Look, Rev. I spent three years in prison? Three years with a bunch of damn numbers for my name, and when I got out I didn't have nothing to hold onto…no ground I could rest my feet firmly upon and say this is a part of me. All I had was a name, a name I didn't recognize anymore—

MCHENRY: Really, Ty, I wish I could help but—

TY: Listen to me, man!

(Pause)

MCHENRY: I'm listening.

TY: When your… Our father came, and put me in charge of that community center. Gave me a purpose. Gave me something to live for.
Every time I open the doors to that place, I see that day he hugged me, placed the keys to that building in my hand. Hear him tell me how he believes in me. I ain't

never had nobody tell me they believe in me till then.
Meant something. I can't lose that building, Reverend.
In those walls, is my soul, I find it in that building do
you understand that. I can't lose that. Cause if I do
then, I lose what our father gave me.
My name back.
And I can't live without it. I'm just asking for a little bit
of help, that's all.

MCHENRY: I might be able to give a small donation.

TY: Well, we would like it if—

MCHENRY: We?

TY: We as in the people—

MCHENRY: How much do you owe?

TY: Few thousand in back taxes.

(Pause)

MCHENRY: A few thousand?!

TY: Maybe more.

MCHENRY: Maybe more?

TY: Okay twenty-three thousand dollars in back taxes.
So, we were hoping that the church—

MCHENRY: The Church—

TY: Our heads under water and we don't know who to
turn to.

MCHENRY: So, you find yourself here.
At the church doorstep hands wide open and
outstretched with full expectation that we'll be more
than willing to pour out our meager coffers to come to
your aid because you and a few others aren't able to
render unto Caesar.

TY: For years the community has been able to depend
on the church—

McHenry: That's beautiful. There's a lot of weight placed upon the church right now. Tell you what… Let's create a repayment plan in which you can pay the church back within a few months and—

Ty: We're struggling Reverend. We go in debt to you then it's just a juggling act for us.

McHenry: You have a better option?

Ty: Yeah…do a charitable act for the community.

McHenry: You can't be serious. Twenty-five thousand dollars, Ty! Charitable act for the community means the church funds suffer. Ty, I'm sorry but we're not going to be able to help you right no.

(Enter MAMA LOVE, she carries a large paper bag.)

MAMA LOVE: *(Sings)*
Oh Jesus is knocking upon your hearts door
Waiting for you to let Him in!
Afternoon Reverend…

McHenry: Does anybody knock anymore?

MAMA LOVE: *(Sings)*
Jesus is knocking on your hearts door
Waiting to free you from all sin!
How you doing Reverend? It does my heart good to see you following after your dad and all. Hey there Ty! How your family and them? Good to see you getting along with your brother. The blood will be united!!!

McHenry: Give me strength. Give me strength.

Ty: Family is fine, Mama Love. How is your son doing?

MAMA LOVE: Sebastian? Whew! Sweet boy, but when the meek inherit the earth he's going to be first in line for some beachfront property.

McHenry: Most importantly. How are you?

MAMA LOVE: Well, my sugar been acting up. I went to that new fancy free clinic that they put up recently and you know some silly lil' white boy doctor tried to put me on some restrictive diet, but I told him the Lord is my guide at all times, and Fried chicken is the gospel bird, what I look like giving up on the Lord's favorite winged animal.

Did you eat, Reverend? Knew you were going to be slaving for the Lord in the Master's house so I figured I'd make you some food.

(MAMA LOVE hands MCHENRY the bag.)

MCHENRY: That's very nice of you, but I was actually planning to go out with my wife later.

MAMA LOVE: No problem at all Reverend, call her over here. I ain't met her yet.

Heard she's beautiful. Skinny but a beautiful little thing. I wanted to welcome you back home, Reverend, so I made enough to put some meat on both your bones. Good Lord Jesus said, 'Man does not live on bread alone.'

So, I made you some fried chicken, some baked chicken, candied yams, mashed potatoes, collard greens, ox tails, and for dessert peach cobbler.

MCHENRY: That's very kind of you, Mama Love. This is too much, thank you…I'm in the middle of a meeting right now. Give me a few, I'll speak with you shortly.

MAMA LOVE: I'll sit right here in this chair while you two gentlemen converse… (Pause) Sit right here…don't mind me—

MCHENRY: So, as I was saying Brother Southmill—

MAMA LOVE: Oh, this is a real nice chair. Need to get a chair with cushioning like this in my house. This is nice. This is real nice—

MCHENRY: So, Brother Southmill…Ty, what I'd like—

MAMA LOVE: Real nice chair dear…we need to get some of these in the pews. You going to get these kind of seats for the pews? This is a lovely chair, where you get this at?—

(MCHENRY *looks at* MAMA LOVE.)

MAMA LOVE: I'm sorry, Reverend. Continue on.

MCHENRY: Thank you, Mama Love. So, as I was saying… Mount Saint Moses was once a friend to this community and still will be. Get back to me, say tomorrow and let's figure something out, alright?

TY: But you just said—

MCHENRY: I know what I said, Ty. If you come by tomorrow perhaps we can figure something out. I got a meeting later today with an old friend and I'll see if she might be of some assistance. I'll talk to you later, Ty.

TY: Take care, Reverend. Mama Love. (*He exits.*)

MCHENRY: Now, Mama Love, what can I do for you? Busy day got to make headway with the Juneteenth Sermon.

MAMA LOVE: Well, I felt a spirit tugging at me this morning, whispering to me that I needed to come by and take a look at you. So here I am.

MCHENRY: Ty asked you to come, didn't he?

MAMA LOVE: We'll just say that I got a vested interested in how this story ends, Reverend. Especially regarding this property. I remember when you was just a baby running around here just as dusty as you can be. Ummhmm, So dusty I could plant seeds in you and grow mustards.
Now look at you, about to give your first Juneteenth sermon.

MCHENRY: I've given sermons before.

MAMA LOVE: Oh, honey. Don't get me wrong. You're sermon last week was nice, tad boring but nice. And let's just be honest, funeral speeches don't count, sweetie. Juneteenth sermon! People come from all over town. Everybody knows about The Prophecy and ready to see it fulfilled. So you got to get this sermon just right, dear! You going to take the sermon from the Book of Matthews? I loved it when your father spoke about Jesus feeding the multitude.

MCHENRY: I was debating—

MAMA LOVE: Your father made that speech every year. I loved those speeches… Talked about the movement, and stepping forward together as a community—

MCHENRY: I was there. But I think I'm going to take the sermon in a different direction this year.

MAMA LOVE: I see.

MCHENRY: Planning to take everything in a new direction. New Preacher… New Image.

MAMA LOVE: I brought you something.

Mama Love pulls out a small leather- bound book.

MAMA LOVE: I think he'd want you to have this.

MCHENRY: His sermon book.

MAMA LOVE: Your father always spoke about the community during Juneteenth. Maybe one of his old sermons might inspire you. Back then was some good old days. Yes indeed, some truly good old times. He'd get up there and roar. Set afire our very souls. Then afterward he'd have all of us go to me and Clarence's house, and we'd have a good old glory glory of a time. Have us a wonderful get together.

MCHENRY: I'm not my old man, Mama Love. I hope you don't expect me to do the same sermons he did.

MAMA LOVE: Let me look at you.

MCHENRY: Mama Love, I have a lot of work to take care of—

MAMA LOVE: Said, let me look at you, preacher. *(Pause)* See, I got this gift, two gifts really, cooking and measuring up the souls of good men. Let me look. Just like I thought. I knew that was him in there hiding.

MCHENRY: Nobody is hiding.

MAMA LOVE: I see your father in you. *(Pause)* …Deep inside of you. *(Pause)* So much of him in you. Alive inside of you. You're going to be our Moses, lead us out of Egypt when the time comes. The prophecy your father put before us was simple. "The blood is to be united, an angel is finally heard, the sheep is to be led, and the multitude is to be fed."

MCHENRY: That prophecy isn't real. I'm my own man. Wish you'd understand that.

MAMA LOVE: "The blood is to be united, an angel is finally heard, the sheep is to be led, and the multitude is to be fed." The prophecy is real, Reverend, it's real. As real as you and me standing here. Your grandfather foretold it. Your father preached it.

MCHENRY: Mama Love, don't confuse me for my father, I am not him, I'm not that lying hypocrite that preached the good book from the Pulpit on Sundays only to turn around and cheat on his wife…on my mother, when no one was looking! A woman that glowed before this congregation countless Sundays only to sneak away in the quiet of the night to kneel on the cold worn tiles of our kitchen to pour out lonesome tears. A perfect man, a perfect marriage. I used to think cancer killed my momma…pretending day to day my father was some great man is what killed her. So no, I'm not him.

MAMA LOVE: Reverend.

MCHENRY: Don't want to hear it! And all that prophecy talk is ridiculous. I don't want to hear no more talk out of you about that.

MAMA LOVE: I see your eyes and within them I see your soul—

MCHENRY: Mama Love.

MAMA LOVE: I see your soul, John McHenry *(Pause)* There is a greatness trying to peak through. And yet there's a shadow over you. I'll pray baby, I'll pray for you. Don't be scared to let your light shine, Preacher. Enjoy the food baby, food for the soul. That's Soul food. Hope that helps fill you and your first lady up nicely. See you in the bye and bye.

MCHENRY: Mama Love?

MAMA LOVE: Yes baby?

MCHENRY: I am not my father.

Mama Love turns to exit and stops.

MAMA LOVE: Reverend, some people come into this building they see four walls, a ceiling over their heads to shelter them from the rain and the weather… but me.

MCHENRY: What do you see?

MAMA LOVE: When I step through these doors into this sanctuary. I hear the heartbeat of those who have gone on before us beating, loud like drums. I hear them whispering your name, I see three generations of McHenry men leading their community. I see two generations of history, two generation of great men that lead us through dark valleys, I look at you and see you leading those sheep through a dark and cruel place, a valley of fog filled with wolves in disguise…I don't rightly know whether or not we'll make it through to the other side of the valley, but I know that you're our shepherd, and just like the rest of the sheep, I will follow you. You're father wasn't a perfect man, nobody is asking for that, he was *a ma*n that knew how to lead us through the darkest of storms. And that is the kind of man we need. So, when you tell me that you're not your father, I got to look at you and say "No and yes" … "yes and no" … Welcome home, Reverend. *(She exits.)*

(Lights shift)

(McHENRY *looks at his father's sermon book he begins working through his sermon.)*

McHENRY: Five fish sticks. Two slices of wonderbread can't feed me let alone a damn multitude. *(He stops momentarily and rips it apart…. He tears up the paper.)*

(CLARE WINTERS *enters. She is a business woman with elaborate tastes for the finer things in life. She's a corporate queen.)*

WINTERS: When they told me John McHenry Jr. was named Preacher for Mount Saint Moses Baptist Church, I couldn't believe it. I said these people must have no clue how much sinning that man has committed in his younger days. The stories I could tell. Memory serves you were oh so very good at it.

McHENRY: A gift and a talent.

WINTERS: You were very talented.

McHENRY: Some of the best preachers were once sinners.

WINTERS: Bet some of the best sinners are preachers.

McHENRY: Well, thankfully the Lord has seen me out.

WINTERS: Ain't that a shame. Hope I haven't come at a bad time?

McHENRY: Not at all, I'm experiencing… Preacher's block.

WINTERS: Sorry to hear that.

MCHENRY: It's to be expected I guess. I'm a month away from the biggest sermon of my career. My father use to say, "Writers block is God's way of keeping you from saying something stupid." So, I'm hoping that's what's happening. It's good seeing you Claire.

*((*MCHENRY *and* WINTERS *hug.)*

(It's a long hug.)

(They part.)

(Silence)

MCHENRY: You look incredible. Is it still Ms Winters?

WINTERS: Still Ms. Winters. Business never gave me the pleasure of settling down. You?

MCHENRY: Newly wed, Two months, now actually, going on three.

WINTERS: Oh, well, I guess congrats is in order.
So? The years have been really, really good to you.

MCHENRY: What's the saying "Black don't crack!"

*(*MCHENRY *and* WINTERS *laugh.)*

(She walks around the sanctuary, surveying the place.)

WINTERS: This is a really nice place you have?

MCHENRY: Small but nice. It could use a renovation, a touch up here and there. Hasn't really been touched since the Eighties. All things in due time, right?

WINTERS: Right. John McHenry, a preacher. Banker, lawyer, doctor, entrepreneur, maybe a politician… but a preacher, whew…never. *(Pause)* How long has it been?

MCHENRY: High School… Eleven years. The memories huh?
You look incredible.

WINTERS: You've said that.

MCHENRY: I wasn't sure if you'd take my call. I've been wanting to talk to you for a while actually.

WINTERS: Why?

MCHENRY: Just how things ended. *(Pause)* Our folks… ugly.

WINTERS: That was the world then but look at us now.

MCHENRY: All grown up.

WINTERS: We decide the rules to play by.

MCHENRY: Of course.
Can I offer you a cup of coffee?

WINTERS: I'd love some.
This really is a lovely church. It has a sense of history. Almost fragile.

MCHENRY: It's been in my family for…two generations, three counting me—

WINTERS: Funny how history is. Thank you, John.

(WINTERS notices that MCHENRY only brought one cup.)

WINTERS: You're not having any?

MCHENRY: No…only had enough for one cup.

WINTERS: That's fine, we can share.

(WINTERS takes a slow sip from the cup and hands it MCHENRY that sips from it as well. He hands it back to her.)

WINTERS: So, what is it that you want from me, Reverend?

MCHENRY: I saw your name in the paper. Thought it was an incredible act of charity putting the free clinic in this neighborhood. I think it's great what you're doing for this community.

WINTERS: And here I was hoping it we could mix business and pleasure.

MCHENRY: Oh—

WINTERS: Relax. So tense… I'm kidding, preacher man. Anyhow. Thank you, John, I'd like to think so. City council meetings lately, the agendas of some of these people are awful. Everybody wants to tear this neighborhood down.

MCHENRY: What do you want?

WINTERS: Build it into what it could be.
Bible says "Therefore encourage one another and build each other up."

(MCHENRY nods.)

MCHENRY: First Thessalonians 5:10…

WINTERS: Chapter 5 verse 11, actually.

(WINTERS sees a Bible and picks it up and hands it to MCHENRY.)

WINTERS: You sure about doing this preacher thing?

MCHENRY: I stand corrected.

(There's a silence between MCHENRY and WINTERS as they pass the coffee cup between each others in an almost ritualized communion. Their eyes meet and he rises from and paces. She looks at him. He looks at her.)

MCHENRY: What are you thinking?

(WINTERS stands close to MCHENRY.)

WINTERS: Remember the beach after prom…the water, the waves crashing against us, laying in the sand, we spent the whole night… Howling at the moon…just me and you.

MCHENRY: You said it was corny.

WINTERS: No, I loved it. It's funny, but I think that might have been the best night of my life.

MCHENRY: You know I never got my deposit back for that tux.

WINTERS: That was a very snazzy tux by the way.

MCHENRY: Seems like a long time ago.
Clare…

WINTERS: So, let's talk business. You sent my office a proposal about opening a school.

MCHENRY: Yes, I did. I hope you realize how important it is to bring a charter school for gifted young men in the arts and sciences is to this neighborhood. It could help everyone in this city.

WINTERS: And you need me because?

MCHENRY: You're a respected real estate developer who sits on city council. Some even go as far as say you are *the city*. With your signature—my school will be approved.

WINTERS: John, are you asking me to back you?

MCHENRY: Look at it as helping a community in need.

WINTERS: Your father's name alone carries enough weight with the city council.

MCHENRY: On a matter of this magnitude the city council isn't going to care who my father was.

WINTERS: It's a gamble. Just a few days ago a guy got murdered a few blocks from here. Your neighborhood, isn't exactly ideal.

MCHENRY: Which is why this school is so necessary.

WINTERS: I believe in what you're doing, I honestly do… But—

MCHENRY: But?

WINTERS: To help you, you're going to have to make it attractive to me.

MCHENRY: So, what is that I can do?

WINTERS: This is business, John, people are going to think I'm crazy if I try to convince them to put their Starbuck's between Big Daddy's Used Tire and Auto Repair and Uncle Reggie's Liquor Emporium. But make it seem like a nice place to move into. A place where change can happen. I'm sure votes can be swayed.

MCHENRY: What do you have in mind?

WINTERS: Time will tell. After all cash is king. How about you put in your proposal for the school and if you aren't able to get it to go through, give me a call. Let's see what we can do. Maybe, if you have some kind of collateral. I don't know. We'll see. I actually have an idea in the works that I think you might be interested in. You scratch my back and I'll scratch yours. I can't help but think there's a reason for us to meet again after all these years. What do you think?

MCHENRY: I would make for a terrible preacher if I didn't think God had something great in store. I'm looking forward to this.

(WINTERS *moves close to* MCHENRY. *Straightens his suitcoat, and smiles.*)

WINTERS: Me too.

(RAYMOND *enters.*)

RAYMOND: Hey Missus, you drive a Red Mercedes?

WINTERS: Yes, that's my car.

RAYMOND: Well, hate to tell you this, but you got some impoverished looking gentleman outside admiring your rims, like they're his next meal ticket.

WINTERS: Think about what we talked about and get in contact with me… *(Shes hurriedly exits.)*

*(*MCHENRY *takes a sip from the cup of coffee.)*

MCHENRY: Deacon Raymond?

RAYMOND: Yeah, boy?

MCHENRY: Nobody was messing with her car.

RAYMOND: Caught me red-handed, *(laughs)* I don't get much entertainment in my old age, moments where I get to see hoity toity people like that squirm, I'm not gonna pass up.

MCHENRY: What am I to do with you?

RAYMOND: I could ask you the same question…What she want?

MCHENRY: Old friend, just handling some business.

RAYMOND: Careful, boy, she wants you to put a little cream in her coffee if you know what I mean.

MCHENRY: I have no clue what that means.

RAYMOND: I'm serious, boy. I'm serious. Cream. Coffee. You think on that.

(End scene)

Interlude

*(*MAMA LOVE *sings, the chorus sings behind* MCHENRY.*)*

MAMA LOVE: *(Sings)*
Jesus is on that mainline
Tell Him what you want
Jesus is on that mainline
Tell Him what you want
Jesus is on that mainline
Tell Him what you want
Call Him up and tell Him what you want

Well, the line ain't never busy
Tell Him what you want
Wo, that line ain't never busy
Tell Him what you want
Well, the line ain't never busy
Tell Him what you want
Keep on calling Him up
And tell Him what you want

Scene Three:
Surviving in Babylon

(A week has passed.)

(MCHENRY stands over a new altar cloth sits over the altar. This one beautiful, made of fine silk it's impressive. He's on the phone.)

MCHENRY: Thank you. I understand. Good afternoon. *(Hangs up)* I can't believe this mess.

(RAYMOND enters.)

RAYMOND: Something a matter, boy?

MCHENRY: Yeah, I live in a world where good blacks suffer because bad ones prosper. The bastards over at the city council told me that because this is a low-income area, "It wouldn't be an ideal site for a school." Can you believe that? "Not an ideal site."

RAYMOND: America created the Babylon. We just have to live in it.

MCHENRY: See, thinking like that is exactly what I'm talking about. We sit here blaming those people for everything when we ought to be looking at ourselves. Look at Ty Southmill. What type of life could he have had if he didn't go to prison? Look at the children around here.

RAYMOND: Excuse me?

MCHENRY: It just pisses me off that I'm trying to promote change within the community and the city isn't helping me cause to them we're just a bunch of niggers!

RAYMOND: What is wrong with you boy? We all got our flock to minister. This is yours.

MCHENRY: Well, that isn't exactly my choice now is it?

RAYMOND: We always have a choice, don't believe otherwise, boy, don't ever believe otherwise. You had the choice to pick up the phone when I called and said your father was dead. You had the choice to come down to the funeral, and you had the choice to take on the role as Reverend of this church. You have a choice, I have a choice, we all have a choice.

MCHENRY: Being trapped here is the only choice I've ever had. I go against my father's wishes and leave Houston. I come back. Leave seminary and go into education. I come back.
It's my curse. As a McHenry.
When I got your phone call that my father was dead, I had this sickening feeling of "the king is dead, long live the king" *(Laughs)* And then when I got to the wake, I stood before this massive casket, to hold this massive man and thought to myself.
This hollow shell use to be a man, he made me, and this is where my father always planned for me to be. Here. Taking up the calling that he took and his father before him did. I cried not because my father was gone, but because I realized I was trapped. I cried so hard I-damn near fell out on the damn casket. I never had a choice just gone through life pretending I did.

RAYMOND: Sad, you think that, boy.

Now your father, now he was a lion of a man. Boy, I haven't seen you roar once. This community needs someone that will roar for them.

McHENRY: Well stick around, you're in for a pleasant surprise. If I can show Ms. Winters, I have enough collateral I can get her backing. That's all I need to make this work. I want you to talk to Ty.

RAYMOND: I don't know Reverend.

McHENRY: He'll listen to you Raymond, talk to him.

(TY *enters.*)

TY: How you doing Deacon Raymond?

Raymond doesn't speak.

Hey what's up, Reverend? You said come back today.

McHENRY: Ty, Deacon Raymond here, says he is waiting for me to roar.

TY: What that mean?

McHENRY: I don't think Deacon Raymond knows that either.

TY: What?

McHENRY: Nothing, inside joke. Ty, I'm glad you came, wanted to talk to you regarding the properties.

TY: I'm all ears, preacher. (*He sits down.*)

McHENRY: Now as I had said before the weight of helping the community center might be too much to bear for the church on it's own. I honestly can't see us just handing you the money.

(TY *prepares to leave.*)

McHENRY: Wait a minute, brother—

TY: Don't you brother me! We ain't blood! I don't care what Mama Love says. That's how you going to do me? I come to you with my hands open and you standin' there this whole time just grinnin' in my face!

RAYMOND: Ty!

TY: Look Rev, I had hoped that you of all people would understand what that community center means.

McHENRY: Hold on now, I'm not done. Mount St. Moses has always been about the community, but I need you to understand this is a business. Now, if you place the deeds of that center and the additional properties in my hand. That's another story. I'll do everything in my capacity as a leader of this community to ease you and the families that take shelter there, of your financial troubles.

TY: So, you're going to help us?

McHENRY: Of course, I'm going to help you. What's the alternative? Foreclose on your property? Or you can sell it to the church and take out of circulation so you don't lose it. The residents facing foreclosure can then continue living the lives you've been living, paying a small sum to the church and we can go from there.

TY: What if?

McHENRY: I don't believe in the "what if?", Ty, your center will be under the loving grace of Mount St. Moses Baptist Church. I'm giving you an offer to save the Center. Think it over, I'll talk to you later.

TY: I'll set up a community meeting and talk it over with them. Thank you, Reverend. I'm sorry about earlier. I'm just...stressed. *(He turns to leave.)*

McHENRY: Oh, Ty, one of the kids left something. I trust you know what to do with this.

(McHENRY goes to the pulpit and hands TY the gun.)

(TY looks first at the gun then towards McHENRY.)

TY: Take care, Reverend.

(TY *exits as* MCHENRY *and* RAYMOND *watch him leave.*)

RAYMOND: Boy, I got a heap load of questions.
What you doing with a gun?

MCHENRY: Long story.

RAYMOND: We can't even afford a security system.
How we going to afford to buy the deeds of not just the
community center but the homes, connected to it? Here
I was thinking all our money went into the bid for the
Academy.

MCHENRY: Going to do a little roaring and hope
someone hears me—

(RAYMOND *looks at* MCHENRY *for a moment and exits.*
Leaving MCHENRY *alone momentarily with his thoughts.*
He pulls out a cell phone from his coat and dials.)

MCHENRY: Hey, Clare, how you doing? This is John.
Yeah, I want to talk to you about something… Yeah…
an interesting idea. Very interesting.

(*End scene*)

Scene Four:
Trouble at Home

(MCHENRY *working on a laptop working on a memo.*
RAYMOND *is busy dusting the piano when* ANGELA *enters,*
Mid-afternoon. RAYMOND *is singing Marvin Gaye's Sexual*
Healing.)

RAYMOND:
When I get that feeling,
I needa sexual healing.
Sexual healing!

MCHENRY: Stop…stop…no more.

RAYMOND: What? Ain't nothing wrong with a little Marvin Gaye.

MCHENRY: Bringing that secular music into God's house.
Ruining that song for me, for life... Anytime I hear it, now, all I'm going to be doing is picturing two old raisins rubbing against each other. Just wrong.

RAYMOND: Boy, what you doing picturing my raisins?

(ANGELA *enters. She's not sure what she just walked into.*)

ANGELA: I can come another time.

MCHENRY: Afternoon, love. Nice to see you—

ANGELA: Really?

MCHENRY: What do you think?

McHenry moves to kiss her, Angela pushes him aside.

ANGELA: How you doing Deacon Raymond?

RAYMOND: Doing fine. How's the most beautiful Angel ever to walk Fourth Ward doing?

ANGELA: I'm doing fine...thought about you earlier, so I brought you Fried Chicken from the soul food restaurant across the street.

MCHENRY: Oh, I'm starving—

ANGELA: Oh, you poor thing, I just got enough here for Deacon Raymond. I knew he'd appreciate it

RAYMOND: Thank you, Angel, you are truly a blessing. (*He reaches into the bucket of chicken begins to eat.*)

MCHENRY: Oh, that's just cruel.

ANGELA: You're in hot water with me. I called up the airline and they told me that it would now cost us $670 for the flight to Chicago for thanksgiving. I need to know one ticket or two.

MCHENRY: Can we do this another time?

ANGELA: You've been stalling for days. For me to get the price, I have to purchase them today.

MCHENRY: Baby, we can't do this right now.

ANGELA: What do you mean?

MCHENRY: I mean we're going to have to wait for a little while, I got our money tied up in the purchase of some property.

ANGELA: You're buying property now? What property? Why didn't you tell me about this?

MCHENRY: It's complicated.

ANGELA: John Edward McHenry Junior, you better un-complicate it!

RAYMOND: Oh! Well will you look at the time… Think I forgot to empty the trash. (He, with chicken in hand, exits quickly.)

MCHENRY: Why you got to call out my full name like that, huh? I told you, I'll talk to you about this later. *(He goes to exit.)*

ANGELA: Don't you walk away from me.

MCHENRY: I don't have time for this, Angela—

ANGELA: Make time, John.

MCHENRY: Angela.

ANGELA: I want to go back home to Chicago, we had a good life. This is going backward not forward and I can't do that…saw people dealing drugs on the corner.

MCHENRY: Drugs are everywhere Angela.

ANGELA: They had guns…guns!

(MCHENRY *laughs*.)

MCHENRY: This is Texas, baby… Everybody has guns…even Old Lady Goody has a gun.

ANGELA: It's not safe here.

McHENRY: This is a good place, baby… Give it some time.

ANGELA: Is this the kind of neighborhood you want your children, to grow up in?

McHENRY: Angela, please—

ANGELA: No, John, you listen to me, this place is consuming you. Look at us. It's tearing us apart, John. Are we even important to you anymore?

McHENRY: I shouldn't have to tell you every second of the day… You know that you're important to me—

ANGELA: Show me.

McHENRY: You'll see.

ANGELA: Am I going to have to wait for the saints to come marching in?

McHENRY: Have you checked with the Women's Auxiliary Board yet?

ANGELA: You mean the Menopause Mafia?!! Telling me how to dress, telling me how a wife should act, and every last one of them wearing a ridiculously big hat… There is no way I'm working with those women. What are we doing here?

(MAMA LOVE *enters quietly watching unnoticed.*
McHENRY *moves towards* ANGELA.)

McHENRY: Look at this altar with its ragged wooden cross and the broken glass in the window. I'm not sure what it's going to cost but I got to make something out of this place. I don't know how to explain it but…I feel…I hear…something beating inside me, beating inside these walls.

ANGELA: Oh, my God, you really want to be here, don't you?

McHENRY: I just know I got to try and make this work…

McHenry's thoughts are interrupted as Mama Love clears her throat announcing her presences.

McHENRY: Afternoon Mama Love.

MAMA LOVE: Let me talk to that pretty misses of yours.

McHENRY: Mama Love?

MAMA LOVE: Alone, preacher.

McHENRY: I'll be…I'll go check on Deacon Raymond. *(He exits.)*

MAMA LOVE: McHenry men. Always trying to swim upstream and don't realize it'll be easier if they turn around and swim down river with the rest of us fish. That's why McHenry men are great men. He'll come around due time…just wait.

ANGELA: I'm sorry ma'am, who are you?

MAMA LOVE: Oh, how rude of me. I'm Sadie May Jenkins, but everybody around here call me Mama Love, baby, and you must be Angela. I've heard lot about you. So glad we finally meeting.

ANGELA: Hopefully they were good things?

MAMA LOVE: You know we church folk like to talk, mostly gossip, but we do talk. Believe me they weren't lying when they said you were a beautiful thing.

ANGELA: Thank you, ma'am.

MAMA LOVE: Skinny…but beautiful. McHenry men love them some beautiful women. We going to hope John not like his daddy in that aspect, but they do love them some beautiful women.

ANGELA: If he were that would explain a lot lately.

MAMA LOVE: Baby, I'm not saying that's how Reverend McHenry is…I'm just saying that he got that gene in him. What you all sad about?

ANGELA: Nothing ma'am… *(Pause)* I should be going now. It was nice speaking with you Mama Love, but I—

MAMA LOVE: Wait a minute now… Let me look at you baby. See I got two gifts in life, cooking and looking into peoples' souls. *(Pause)* Come here baby, let me look into your eyes. Interesting…Very interesting.

ANGELA: What?

MAMA LOVE: Oh, nothing.

ANGELA: What is it?

MAMA LOVE: Nothing at all. Just a little something that caught my attention is all. Old age getting to me. Probably didn't see what I thought I saw.

ANGELA: What was it?

MAMA LOVE: Oh, you don't want to hear an old lady chatterin' on.

ANGELA: Is there something wrong?

MAMA LOVE: Well…it's just that I see his father in him, but I see his son in you.*(Pause)* He doesn't know does he?

ANGELA: How?

MAMA LOVE: I got two gifts, baby.

ANGELA: You saw that just by looking at me? How did you know?

MAMA LOVE: That's not important. What is however is you, sweetheart. How come you haven't told him yet?

ANGELA: I've tried—

MAMA LOVE: And you need to try again.

ANGELA: I don't even know if I want this baby.

MAMA LOVE: Any particular reason?

ANGELA: I'm not sure I even know where I'm standing.

MAMA LOVE: Don't know where you standing, baby? You in a church, baby.

ANGELA: I'm talking about where I'm standing in this life and if…if…if I don't know where I stand, how am I going to teach my child where they stand?

MAMA LOVE: You're in Houston, baby, that's where, you standing—

ANGELA: That's not what I meant, Mama Love— I don't know where I'm standing with John, or—

MAMA LOVE: Silence. Silence, baby. That's a McHenry child inside you. McHenry men are an interesting kind of seed… You see they grow best in rough soil and turn into strong Cypress Trees. They grow when our people need to be lead out of Egypt, they don't realize it until the right moment comes, but that's when they suppose to come. Just remember this, behind every great man, behind every great moment in history, right behind them there is a Black woman with a mop. Now I know we just met, but Mama Love wants you to do something. I want you to do something not for me, but for you… If you do, God is going to use you in ways you'd never imagine.

ANGELA: What?

MAMA LOVE: I'm thinking you want to go home and take something that you hold most dear and place that object into the center of a cobbler.

ANGELA: I don't know how to make cobbler.

MAMA LOVE: Well you better learn, sweetheart… Now, once you've placed it into that cobbler, I want you to

take it down to Old Lady Goody before the next full
moon and present it to her as an offering.

ANGELA: Offering?

MAMA LOVE: Did I say offering? I meant gift.

ANGELA: That Crazy Old Voodoo woman?!! The old
lady that shoots at the moon?

MAMA LOVE: Don't doubt what you don't understand.
God has many names and many churches, Black folks
have always served God sweetheart, just in a different
way than them preachers preach about all the time
on Sunday morning. But it was always God… It was
always God… Now you take that cobbler over to Old
Lady Goody; she'll help you figure out where you're
standing.

(End scene)

Scene Five:
To Protect and Serve

*(WINTERS enters carrying an envelope and a tray with two
cups of corporate coffee. She finds MCHENRY sitting ready
for her.)*

MCHENRY: How you doing, Clare?

WINTERS: I've been looking forward to seeing you
again.

MCHENRY: Feeling is more than mutual.

WINTERS: I brought you some coffee…you gave me the
last of yours, figured a nice gesture would be for me
bring you some.

MCHENRY: That's very kind of you.

WINTERS: What are friends for… How's that sermon?

McHENRY: A nightmare. Can't get beyond the first line… Heard you bought the old Guzman Motel.

WINTERS: Lofts. That is where the future lives. Remember I told you that.

McHENRY: I definitely will.

Winters takes a seat.

WINTERS: You know, Reverend, everybody I mean everybody wants a luxury loft near downtown. Just a fifteen minute walk and you're at work…everything your soul could want at your fingertips. Real estate is where the power lies in this world… Buy cheap sell big.

McHENRY: I've been approached purchase some property. A community center and the lands around it…actually.

WINTERS: You should. Property…equals cash and cash is…

McHENRY: Is king…

WINTERS: Good boy.

McHENRY: I remember you had told me that if I had some collateral you'd help me bring my school into this community.

WINTERS: I said I'd help you apply for the Minority Redevelopment Grant.

McHENRY: Yeah, that's where the problem comes in… money troubles.

WINTERS: What money troubles?

McHENRY: Most of my funds are tied into this school… I'm not sure I'm going to have enough to purchase the property.

WINTERS: I could help you cover that…it's not a problem. I'll count it as a nice little tax write-off.

McHENRY: A tax write-off?

WINTERS: I don't know, Throw it… Twenty percent of everything you get back on your investments sounds fair right. Maybe you can name the center after my company. Just think of it as a favor… we're friends… We'll create a joint corporation. You can apply for the Minority Redevelopment Contract and even leave the properties in your name if that would make you feel more comfortable. I'll have my attorneys draw up the paper work and bring it by sometime later.

McHENRY: I'm hesitant.

WINTERS: Other than this shining beacon, this neighborhood is a blight to the city. The majority stake is in your hands, most landlords in the area want to exit, city council all but ready to sign off. The banks and the city are looking for any excuse let go or the property. I'll take care of everything for you. It'll be easy. Painless.

(Silence)

McHENRY: Alright you have yourself a deal.

(McHENRY and WINTERS shake hands.)

(The sound of shattered glass causes her to rise. McHENRY remains seated.)

WINTERS: My car! *(She exits.)*

McHENRY: Nope, that would be the sound of my new window. *(He exits.)*

Scene 6:
Bless Me Now

(A few days have passed. Afternoon. The sound of singing is heard in the distance before RAYMOND enters with a broom, TY enters, hugs RAYMOND, he has an envelope in his hand.)

RAYMOND: *(Sings)*
Bless me now,
Oh gentle savior
Hear my humble cry
(End singing)

(MCHENRY enters the church as RAYMOND is sweeping the pulpit floor. TY sits by the altar.)

MCHENRY: Someone busted out the window again. Afternoon, Ty… *(Pause)* Three times that window has been broken.

RAYMOND: I had forgot to tell you I caught the fella this time.

MCHENRY: You caught him?!!

RAYMOND: Yep, Caught em' red-handed… Caught them while they were in the act.

MCHENRY: Why didn't you tell me this before?

RAYMOND: I told you…I forgot.

MCHENRY: Did you call the police?

RAYMOND: So they can abuse him, cage him up, murder him? They got their justice system…we got ours. It was that old fool that's always walkin' around talking in rhymes and riddles…dirty lookin'… What's his name?

TY: Goes by Rasta?

RAYMOND: That's the one! Anyhow, that's the one that did it.

MCHENRY: Why the hell—

RAYMOND: Blessed are the gentle Lord…blessed are the gentle. You plan to be doing all that swearing during your sermon?

MCHENRY: I've been working on it…did you ask him why he kept busting out our windows?

RAYMOND: Sure did.

MCHENRY: And?

RAYMOND: Told me he was trying to get your attention so he could warn you that the serpent was loose, and it was time that the first to be last and the last first.

MCHENRY: Serpent is loose and the first is last? What? What does that mean?

RAYMOND: Don't ask me, I don't speak "crazy nigga". You asked me what he said; you didn't ask me to interpret it. I told him that we appreciate the warning and he can go ahead and break the window this time, but if he broke another window he was going to be first in line to catch this foot up his behind.

MCHENRY: Deacon Raymond, so you just… let him break the window?

RAYMOND: He was trying to get your attention.

MCHENRY: Well, next time someone wants my attention, how about you give them my phone number.

RAYMOND: Oh, by the way, Southmill is here…

MCHENRY: I can see that.

RAYMOND: Well, I can see that you see that. I'm just letting you know that since its three P M and your meeting time is from ten to two, I should tell you.

MCHENRY: Thank you for your concern, Deacon.

RAYMOND: Believe me no concern at all. None whatsoever…

(MCHENRY *turns his attention to* TY *and the envelope that's in his possession.*)

MCHENRY: My brother, Southmill, How's our neighborhood philosopher doing today?

TY: I'm doing alright… How are you and your number one doing?

MCHENRY: My what?

TY: Your number one… You're wife?

MCHENRY: We're doing good… She took up baking all of a sudden. Not that I mind, but it's just odd. She never baked a day in her life, till she got down here and all of a sudden she's on some mission to bake the perfect cobbler. Makes no sense to me…but the more she bakes the more I eat. Doesn't bother me in the least bit. What do you think that means when a woman suddenly takes up a hobby out of nowhere?

TY: I don't try to understand me no black women. Their minds are like a river, deeper than we can fathom. Their beautiful to look at, but don't swim in it unless you prepared to drink deep or you gonna drown.

(Pause)

MCHENRY: Street philosopher, indeed. Do you have the paperwork for me?

TY: I got it.

Ty pulls out the manila envelope

MCHENRY: Are the deeds signed over correctly?

TY: Just as instructed.

MCHENRY: Well then let me see it.

TY: Reverend…I don't know about this.

MCHENRY: About what?

TY: About this. Me handing over these deeds puts a lot of power into your hands. That's a good deal of power over peoples' lives who don't have anything else to hold on to.

MCHENRY: I'm aware of that Bro. Southmill *(Pause)* Ty?

TY: Yeah, John?

McHENRY: Let me see those deeds.

RAYMOND: You know, I've lived in this world for a long time… I realize looking back that where we were, and where we are now is a lot better than it was; and where we are now is not where God almighty wants us to end. Now I got faith that the preacher understands the trust this community is placing upon his shoulders. Ain't that right, boy?

McHENRY: That's correct.

RAYMOND: Hand the Reverend, the deeds. He's not going to let something bad happen to his flock. After all, he's here to protect the community.

McHENRY: Ty, I'll keep this safe.

TY: You know your old man, I always thought of as father to me. Helped out my mom. Ever since I could remember there was always Deacon Raymond and the Reverend in my life, guiding me…letting me know that in this life I wasn't alone… I used to see you everyday in church and wish I had your life. Use to picture what my life would have, could have been like…Now, I found that all along that's exactly what you were… funny ain't it? Promise you'll keep these safe.

(TY *hands the deed over to* McHENRY *with hesitation.*)

McHENRY: Nothing happen to that center. Have a little faith in me.

(TY *shakes hands and exits.*)

(McHENRY *calls on cell.*)

McHENRY: Clare, how are you doing? Good… that's good. I'm set to get the property appraised. Could you bring by the paperwork on that Minority Redevelopment Grant Project?
Yes…yes…

(*Lights fade*)

(McHenry *stands at the pulpit*

END OF ACT ONE

Interlude

(Spotlight on McHenry *standing at the pulpit.)*

McHenry: It's a glorious morning!
Oh, I will rejoice and be glad in it.
Can I get an Amen, up in here?!!
Today, church, I need to talk to you.
Today, church, if it's alright with you,
I want to talk to you about a dream I've had.
I'd like to talk to you about your glorious future.
Let me hear you say "glorious future!"
Brothers and Sisters, I want to talk to you about the
Minority Redevelopement Grant.

How many of you hold property deeds? How many of
you want to be rich?

(End scene)

(Intermission)

ACT TWO

Scene One:
Waiting For That Lion To Roar

(End of May. Three days prior to full moon. Afternoon)

(MCHENRY works on his sermon. He tosses paper on the floor and begins writing another— before tossing.)

RAYMOND: You know they're turning the Old Guzman Motel into luxury lofts. Luxury lofts.

MCHENRY: I heard.

RAYMOND: Luxury Lofts, a place people like me would never get to step inside—being built in my own neighborhood. It's a cold-blooded move, Reverend. Them people once upon a time didn't want nothing to do with this part of town, now this is prime real estate. Oh, they smart.

MCHENRY: Deacon Raymond?

RAYMOND: Yeah, boy?

MCHENRY: Who are *they*?

RAYMOND: They know who they is? How you going to ask me who *they* is? Everybody know who *they* is?

MCHENRY: What about my wife? Do you consider her one of your *"theys"*?

RAYMOND: No, she's one of "them." There is a difference between a "they" and a "them", boy,

Everybody knows that. Not everyone of "them" is a "they". I like *"them"*, *"they"* on the other hand—I don't trust.

MCHENRY: The Guzman Motel is just the sign of the times. Change has to happen eventually.

RAYMOND: See your, father, he wouldn't have said that. Not your father! Your father would have put up a fight. Been like a lion and roared. Would have yelled to the top of his lungs that "This is our home and it ain't for sale! It ain't for sale!" But you say, "sign of the times." Something is sick inside of you. A sheep coming from a family of lions.

I say you know they're building lofts out of the Old Guzman, sell a loft to those white people for two hundred thousand to five hundred and fifty thousand dollars… You know what I could do with that? For a space that's probably the length of the distance from the baptismal pool to the pulpit box. Next somebody buys the Deli shop that the old Muslims own. Tear that down to put up a Starbucks. And in the end, the neighborhood that once looked like you, isn't going to look like you anymore. They going to be walkin' and talkin' like Ms Winters— except they're holding in one hand a cup of mocha latte with their little high dollar mutt named Mr Muffley in the other.

You ain't going to work that into your sermon, alert the people of the invasion coming? Tell us this Juneteenth to hold fast. None of that touches your nerve, or do the wolves gathering around even phase you.

MCHENRY: I can't stand in the way of progress, Raymond. Nobody can stand in the way.

RAYMOND: Is that what it is? Progress, huh? Blessed are those that suffer. Lord, blessed are those that suffer—

MCHENRY: So you telling me you wouldn't like a Starbucks in this neighborhood?

RAYMOND: Lord forgive me for saying this but my black ass don't give a damn about no Starbucks. *(Turns to leave)* Hey boy, Brother Clarence stopped by earlier, told me Sadie May Jenkin's wants to know what you want to eat for the Juneteenth ceremony. They seem pretty excited about you taking over for your father and—

McHENRY: And?

RAYMOND: You going to let them erase us?

McHENRY: What do you believe?

RAYMOND: I don't rightly know what to believe. When I served this church under your father, I believed in a lot of things. Believed in a lot of dreams. I would kill for those dreams but with you, with you preacher, I don't think I'm going to believe it until I see it.

McHENRY: Then don't.

RAYMOND: That's all you got to say?

McHENRY: Have a little faith in me. I got plans that will take this church to another level. Combine business with church like it should be done. Take this church to a level my father never dreamed of.

RAYMOND: Selling goods in the temple. That's Pharisee talk, Preacher. Jesus smashed up those merchants who sold their goods in the temple. Think on that. Bible says "No one can serve two masters, for you will hate one and love the other, or be devoted to one and despise the other. You can not serve both God…"

McHENRY: "And money," Matthew 6:24… Say what you got to say Deacon.

RAYMOND: Don't know what your intentions are buying up that Community Center. I tell you this much, I know I don't like it.

MCHENRY: Then why you help convince Bro. Southmill to hand over those deeds?

RAYMOND: 'Cause when you accepted the position to be the Reverend, you took on the burden of that cross. My job is to support you as you do it. Whether I agree whatever road you take to get to the hilltop, I'll support you, but I want to put this on the table, after whatever business you choose to go about. You remember the boy that came in here and handed you the gun?

MCHENRY: His name was—

RAYMOND: Elijah. His name *is* Elijah Black. *Is*... not every young man in these streets is dead.

MCHENRY: They call him Jah.

RAYMOND: Boys like him got it hard; don't got nobody to call on. Nobody but Ty Southmill and his Community Center. Who do you think they're going to turn to if something happen to that center?

MCHENRY: He came here to the church.

RAYMOND: He came to the church because someone at that Center told him he should. I tell you this much, the community can't rely on just the church to guide them, especially the young. They have to know that there is more than one thing out there that will always serve and protect them. One is this church— and the other is that Center. You need to reach out to Ty. One teaches to the lost, but the other finds them. We need both here.
Elijah is just like Ty was—angry at the world, angry at life, and for damn good reason. And if your father hadn't reached out to him, that anger would've swallowed him like that big fish did Jonah.

MCHENRY: Raymond, I'm getting that property appraised and then wait till the Lord reveals himself.

But whatever it is it'll be incredible. *(He returns to working diligently on his speech.)*

RAYMOND: How's that speech coming?

MCHENRY: With only five fish, and two loaves how can we feed the multitude?

(Silence)

RAYMOND: Where's the rest of it?

MCHENRY: All I got so far…

RAYMOND: Wish more sermons where short like that.

(RAYMOND exits. Expensive car sound. RAYMOND enters again, checking his watch.)

RAYMOND: Looks like Lil Miss Fancy Pants here to see you?

MCHENRY: Thank you.

RAYMOND: What's with you and that lady anyway?

MCHENRY: We have history.

RAYMOND: I don't trust her.

MCHENRY: She's a good woman. Known her since I was young. Went to this church.

RAYMOND: That don't mean nothing.

MCHENRY: Miss Beulah Winters is her mama. Use to be head of the Ushers Board.

RAYMOND: That still don't mean nothing.

MCHENRY: She can quote scripture better than anyone I know?

RAYMOND: Even the devil can quote scripture, boy.

MCHENRY: I give up.

RAYMOND: You know, I don't speak badly about people, boy. It's 2:02—do you want me to send her away? I can tell her to come back another time; in fact it'll be a pleasure to kick this woman out. Really, it's no problem for me at all.

McHENRY: A little quick to judge aren't you?

RAYMOND: Call them how I see 'em.

McHENRY: Blessed are the poor lord. Blessed are the poor.

RAYMOND: Alright, mock me then.

(WINTERS enters.)

(Exit RAYMOND.)

(She carries a briefcase and a Starbucks coffee cup in the other.)

McHENRY: Clare, thank you so much for meeting with me.

WINTERS: What are friends for? Let's talk. *(She presents a proposal.)* I like your vision for this place, this area. You're a man with a vision. Backing you for the Charter school shows that I believe in you.

McHENRY: It's just one step to my dream fulfilled.

WINTERS: I'm glad you said that word, dreams. I have dreams too. I see a city of gold, and in the center of that city… In Fourth Ward, I see a church that had the foresight to push it towards change. When you picture one image that gives you hope for the future, one tangible image what comes to mind?

McHENRY: Beautiful church with a school adjacent to it. A community, my people can look at and say that their proud.

WINTERS: We can make that dream—together me and you. John, I want to talk to you about what we will call the Fourth Ward Redevelopment Project. It'll prove lucrative beyond our wildest imagination. We can make this the church—the church of the city. The beacon of hope and change this city needs. *(She pulls out the documents.)* The document to get you there. Because of your recent investments in the property of this blighted community, Reverend, the city has no way of denying you a little thing that's called the Minority Redevelopment Grant. This contract can help you acquire that charter school.

McHENRY: And this does what?

WINTERS: Makes you and your church, very wealthy. Remember the golden rule… "Cash is king."

McHENRY: And how exactly do you benefit?

WINTERS: Besides betterment of the neighborhood, which I believe both of us are eager to see—I simply want my realty company to be a chief backer. It helps me by placing stakes in this prime redevelopment sector of the city. Together we develop this community into the newest hot spot of the city. Turn it into the New Harlem of Texas. I'm not going to lie, "Cash is king," John.

McHENRY: Cash is king.

WINTERS: Exactly. Allow me to show you something I've been working on. I brought these blueprints. Here take a look. *(Unrolls blueprints)*

McHENRY: What is this?

WINTERS: For now it's just a proposal, a dream of mine; like you have a dream—I have mine. This is the first step. The Houston Central City Lofts. And look at this …take a look at this, built adjacent to the lofts will be McHenry Park –named after the man who helped begin the New Fourth Ward. A man at a certain point has to ask himself, "What's going to be his legacy?" I'm telling you this is it. Right here on this contract is where it all begins. Reverend John McHenry, The Father of Redevelopment.

MCHENRY: Father of Redevelopment.

WINTERS: Sounds good doesn't? All you have to do is sign this paper, place the mortgages under the company, and change will begin.

(Pause. MCHENRY looks towards the raggedy wooden cross.)

MCHENRY: Do you believe in signs, Clare?

WINTERS: Not quite sure.

MCHENRY: The Lord presents himself in strange ways…

WINTERS: What's wrong?

MCHENRY: My pen is dead.

(ANGELA enters.)

ANGELA: I'm sorry. Was I interrupting anything?

MCHENRY: Just finishing up some last minute business. I'll be right back.

(MCHENRY leaves ANGELA, alone with WINTERS. They stare. Silence)

WINTERS: So you must be the darling preacher's wife.

ANGELA: Yes, ummm…hi…I'm Angela.

WINTERS: Claire.

ANGELA: It's nice to meet you.

WINTERS: Same. You know I don't know if your husband, ever told you— but we grew up together.

ANGELA: You did?

WINTERS: Oh, yes, back then he was…quite the catch. I'm looking at him now and well…I guess somethings just don't change.
You better hold on to that man tight. A man like that is likely to slip from your fingers if you're not careful.

ANGELA: Excuse me?

WINTERS: I don't believe I stuttered, dear.
You seem like a sweet *girl*, but he's a good *man*.
Some *woman* would be quick to try and snatch him away.
You should just keep that in mind.
Hope you taking care of that man.
Good care of him.

(MCHENRY *enters with a pen.*)

MCHENRY: A pen!
I miss something?

WINTERS:	ANGELA:
No.	No.

MCHENRY: Angela, babe what did you come by for?

ANGELA: Nothing…nothing…I'm late. I need to be going.

MCHENRY: Angela?

(ANGELA *leaves.*)

MCHENRY: What was that all about?

WINTERS: You never know with us women. Where were we?

MCHENRY: So, I've been doing some thinking and…
I'm going to place both the community center and the church deeds down for collateral.

(MCHENRY *signs the contract that* WINTERS *presents him and hands it back.*)

WINTERS: Reverend, they're going to thank you for this.

MCHENRY: I know they will.

(MCHENRY *walks* WINTERS *out.*)

(*He returns jubilant.*)

MCHENRY: Yes, yes, yes… This is wonderful. My eyes have seen the coming of the glory of the Lord, baby!

(RAYMOND *enters.*)

RAYMOND: Boy, what are you shouting about?!!

MCHENRY: My dream. If you don't believe, you better start. Mount Saint Moses Missionary Baptist Church is going to be bigger than ever. Deacon, I'm telling you right now, that Juneteenth is going to mean more than just the commemoration of black people's freedom. It's going to mean wealth for this community. Deacon Raymond, as soon as I can break ground, this church is going to boast it's the home of the John McHenry Christian Academy for the Arts and Sciences. So, start believing.

RAYMOND: Your old man would be proud.

MCHENRY: Think so huh? And that's just the beginning. If everything comes together at this meeting Saturday, in two weeks…things will really start happening. The church is going will be amazed.

RAYMOND: A school to educate the children. Now that's what I call a true blessing. Yeah your father would be real proud of you. I can honestly say…I'm proud of you…boy.

MCHENRY: Thank you. Raymond.
How come you stand by me?
You don't even like me but you stand by me…why?

RAYMOND: Reverend…I was once a sinful man. I went to this party, a real sinful party. Whew, that party was sinful… boy, I tell you. The women that was at that party was… sinful; and I was a sinful man at this sinful party. There was liquor there…and drugs at the party, lots of drugs; whole lot of drugs…the heavy kind of drugs and I was greedy. Looking back at it I'd say I was a greedy, sinful man, anyway at this party I got so

greedy I fell out. Fell out so hard, they thought I was
dead… Now the type of people that I was associating
myself with at the time was sinful people. With me
blacked out and all they didn't want the laws to be
coming their direction with them having a lot of illegal
things in they're possession. So they did what anybody
that was sinful and didn't want to get caught in the act
of being sinful does. They left me in the garbage heap
in an alleyway for dead. When I woke up standing
above me, with his hands outstretched reaching down
to help me was your father. The way God's glorious
sun was shining around him, made it look like he wore
a halo… thought he was Jesus at first, come to take me
to hell. I was like I knew Jesus was black… and your
dad, said…"Come on. I want you to walk with me."
…and I said 'who me?' and he helped me up and said
"Yeah, you… You see me talking to anybody else?
Come on. I want you to walk with me." And walk with
him I did. He fed me, he ministered to me…and he
prayed for me. He told me that he needed a man like
me to stand beside him in the hard times that were
going to come… Now, I didn't know why he'd want
me, a sinful man to walk beside him so I told him I'd
cramp his style. You know what he said.

MCHENRY: What he say?

RAYMOND: He said Brother, I got enough style to share
and still be the toughest preacher man in town. That's
when I knew…I'd follow that man to the frontlines
of hell when the great war of Judgment comes, and
heaven, if the Lord ever blesses me to go to the great
beyond. On his deathbed he asked me to watch after
you…he asked me to watch after the Southmill boy.
I guess I did better with one then the other…but
that's what I did. I follow after you now, cause if I
squint, and tilt my head a little to the left, I see your
father inside of you…living. *(Pause)* I see it in you…

the possibilities for it to happen but I wonder if I'll live long enough to see you become a warrior, a king amongst men. Fulfill the prophecy. Hope I can one day look at you and tell myself that's a man... That's a man I'd kill for.

MCHENRY: Why does everybody seem to believe in this prophecy?

RAYMOND: The prophecy is real, preacher. Trust me I know. Why you think your father got me watching after you and Southmill? You two are like this coin I got here, two sides. Going to lead us out of Egypt. Just got to reach out and help Ty up first.

MCHENRY: How?

RAYMOND: Every coin has two sides to it. *(He exits.)*

(MCHENRY goes to his speech before he crosses to the piano. He plays a gentle gospel hymn, which transforms into a hip-hop rhyme, the pace builds up to a hype head-banging frenzy.)

(He realizes ANGELA is standing before him.)

MCHENRY: Baby, you scared me to death. How long have you been standing there?

ANGELA: Long enough to watch you remix, Amazing Grace.

MCHENRY: Ah...yeah well... *(Pause)* I'm glad you're here. I got great news to share. Oh, have you met with the Women's Auxiliary Board yet? I need to get everything finalized for the Juneteenth Service as soon as possible.

ANGELA: I'm not meeting with those crazy old women again. Why don't you call them instead of jamming out, to Run DMC greatest gospel hits?

MCHENRY: Not again please.

(Silence)

ANGELA: Why are you doing this? And don't give me tradition and family prophecy or cryptic visions. The truth.

MCHENRY: I'm hollow inside, Angela. And I got to figure out a way to fill myself. When the school in Chicago was going under, I poured out till I didn't have nothing left. I'd come home to you and hold you, but still...hollow. First time I stepped back in here—for a moment—I felt filled to the brim overflowing.

ANGELA: Hollow... with me? Is that why you stay here so late?

MCHENRY: I love you, but my life...my vessel still feels empty. Beat—hollow. Like a drum Baby. I walk this earth trying to figure out what kind of man I am—that I'm not my father. Went as far as I can go and still find myself right back here...hoping to God after my father died that I'd be able to find—.

ANGELA: You feel hollow with me? It's a simple yes or no.

MCHENRY: If you ride this out with me baby, I know I can...I can—

(ANGELA *touches* MCHENRY's *chest.*)

ANGELA: I'm tired. Why am I fighting for this relationship when you can't see past your self? Tell me, why? I support you. I supported you when you wanted to go into teaching? I supported you when you wanted to come to this awful place... (*Beat*) I talked to my mom, she told me I can come stay with her for a while. Figure out what kind of life I'm willing to live, and what I'm willing to sacrifice. She bought me two tickets. I don't know what you're going to do—but I'm going back to Chicago in two weeks.

MCHENRY: Before my Juneteenth sermon?

ANGELA: I love you, but— (*She takes out two plane tickets.*) If this marriage means anything at all— (*She places one on the altar.*)

MCHENRY: Your home is here.

(MCHENRY *places ticket back into* ANGELA's *hand.*)

MCHENRY: Here with me. Making this place better.

ANGELA: You don't make the ghetto better. You either bulldoze it and start over –or leave it and don't look back.

MCHENRY: Angela…baby. Wait.
Babe, I need you. What else do you want me to say?

ANGELA: Good night, John.

(MCHENRY *flashes their sign.*)

(ANGELA—*two pounds to her heart, peace signs…and then flick him off.*)

(*She leaves.*)

MCHENRY: Damn. (*He sits down by the altar and… screams.*)

(*End scene*)

Scene Two:
Full moon out

(*A week later. Late at night*)

(MCHENRY *stands before the altar picks up the platinum cross admiring it, then notices* MAMA LOVE.)

MCHENRY: Mama Love. What are you doing here so late?

MAMA LOVE: Looking at you…Preacher, why do you hate this church so much? You want to change everything around here? Change the chair the preacher sits in, change the cross that's been sitting on that altar since the genesis of this church

MCHENRY: Mama Love, nothing is wrong with change. Change is a necessity, a part of life, every minute we live is a change.

MAMA LOVE: I use to work in this church answering the phones, scrub these floors, handling the paperwork that would gather on your father's desk…Sometimes work here late till the night would come. And I'd see your father where you standing now. Arms outstretch, sweat and tears pouring down his face. See him talking, not to himself—but to a strong unseen presence, that was within him…that was within these walls—that's within you as well. You hear it, don't you? Why you don't answer it?

MCHENRY: I don't know what you mean.

MAMA LOVE: You left here to escape it.

MCHENRY: But I came back, Mama Love. I'm standing here right now! Came back to help the community… nothing more…I don't believe in any prophecies…all of that is foolishness.

MAMA LOVE: Come here preacher.
Come here.

(MCHENRY *moves to* MAMA LOVE…)

MAMA LOVE: Hold this.

(MAMA LOVE *hands* MCHENRY *an envelope.*)

(*She slaps him.*)

MAMA LOVE: Me and my neighbors got told by Ty Southmill we got to leave our homes, Reverend? Why I got to leave the place, I've been resting my weary bones down at? Why the Community Center they got to close their doors? Cause your bettering the community? Cause change is a necessity? That letter telling me that I got to leave my home, Reverend. To think, I was looking forward to seeing what the good Lord did with you.

MCHENRY: I don't know anything about a letter.

MAMA LOVE: Sellin' us for cheap…in the name of change. These streets are spiritual…our lives…our homes…our memories, spiritual. Torn down to be replaced by profit?
Do you see us?

(MCHENRY *opens it and reads*.)

MCHENRY: McHenry-Winters Redevelopment…legal …ownership…the deed of your property…hereby requests that you vacate… *(Pause)* Vacate your home… Mama Love, I did not approve this. I promise you—

MAMA LOVE: Your name is on it ain't it?

MCHENRY: Yeah but—

MAMA LOVE: You tell me something Reverend. You tell me how you going to preach this Sunday about Juneteenth and freedom— when you selling ours?

MCHENRY: This must be a mistake.

MAMA LOVE: It damn well better be.

MCHENRY: Let me take care of this, I'll make sure everything gets right.

MAMA LOVE: Lived all my life to see you make things "right." What we say when the whites move back into the wards they once upon a time didn't want? Oh, "Time to move!" Move to where? Not the suburbs, can't afford it there. Not into some fancy lofts can't afford it there! No choice but to just fade away.

MCHENRY: I've got a duty to shepherd this flock and that's what I'm going to do.

MAMA LOVE: If the wolves take us all in the night while you sleep, Reverend—what sheep you going to shepherd?

McHENRY: This wasn't suppose to happen. Not like this. *(He dials cell. On phone)* This is Reverend McHenry calling for Ms Winters, I'm told that residents of this neighborhood are being harassed with letters of eviction. This wasn't a part of the Redevelopment Project and unless you retract --I'm pulling my name off the contract. *(Hangs up)* This is simply a misunderstanding—

MAMA LOVE: It damn right better be a misunderstanding!

McHENRY: Mama Love please…I just need you to have a little faith.

(Gunshot. Silence. Gunshot)

(McHENRY and MAMA LOVE stare towards gun fire.)

McHENRY: Mama Love?

MAMA LOVE: Eight fourteen, Reverend. Full moon.

McHENRY: Old Lady Goody never shoots her gun twice at the moon. As long as I've lived, I don't think she's ever shot it twice.

MAMA LOVE: Where your wife tonight, Reverend?

McHENRY: Asleep. At home.

MAMA LOVE: Reverend…I wouldn't be so sure of that. *(Beat)* Can you feel that Reverend?

McHENRY: Feel what?

MAMA LOVE: The heart beat of the ancestors rejoicing. The passing on of the light.

(RAYMOND enters the church with ANGELA, his arm wrapped around her as he leads her inside.)

MAMA LOVE: A new priestess for the people has been chosen. *(She sits down on the floor, staring off vacantly, singing an ancient African lullaby.)*

RAYMOND: Found her out there with Old Lady Goody. Gun in her hand waving it around like crazy at the moon. Howling and speaking in tongues. When we got there –she looked right through me. I ain't never been looked at like that before. She looked right through me into my soul. I'm telling you something is wrong with her.

MAMA LOVE: Nothing is wrong with her. God is using her.

MCHENRY: Angela? Angela? Why isn't she talking?

MAMA LOVE: Sometimes God's mystery takes time to work through the system… *(She reaches to comfort her.)*

MCHENRY: Don't touch her. You knew this would happen. *(Pause)* Is this God's will? *We* shouldn't have come here. Baby, I'm sorry. Please say something… just say something.

McHenry wraps his arms around her.

MAMA LOVE: "The blood is to be united, an angel… heard, the sheep…led, and the multitude…to be fed." This is all a part of the prophecy.

MCHENRY: I don't believe in the prophecy. Angela. Speak to me. Angela, baby, say something.

*(*ANGELA *says nothing.)*

*(*MCHENRY *picks her up.)*

MAMA LOVE: Reverend? Can you feel them? Can you feel them talking to you?

MCHENRY: Angela?

*(*MCHENRY *exits carrying* ANGELA.*)*

MAMA LOVE: *(Sings)*
Amazing Grace, How sweet the sound
That saved a wretch like me
I once was lost, but now am found
T'was blind but now I see

(End scene)

Scene Three:
This is my home, and it's not for Sale.

(Morning, two days later)

*(*McHENRY *sits by the altar studying documents.)*

*(*RAYMOND *enters.)*

RAYMOND: Morning, boy.

McHENRY: Morning.

RAYMOND: Has she talked at all?

McHENRY: It's been two days and she hasn't said a thing at all. Just looks at me. And if she doesn't look at me, she stares out the window pointing towards Sis. Jenkins house. I'm worried about her. I just don't know what to do.

RAYMOND: Things will work out boy, rest on that.

*(*TY *storms and tosses a crumpled ball of paper at* McHENRY.*)*

TY: You slick ass nigger...!

RAYMOND: Ty! This is the Lord's house!

TY: What about the people? Suppose to be room in the Lord's house for the people. All our life hearing "in the Lord's house is many mansions" Where's mine? Where's the peoples?
Supposed to be where we can go when there is nowhere else...

You preach prosperity— but only one prospering is
you. Claim to heal our souls but only suck the life
out. Where we suppose to turn to now, huh? This is
supposed to be our house too!

MCHENRY: This is your house…

TY: A house of lies. This is the home of a blonde hair,
blue eyed Jesus, taking up residence in the hood, cause
it's convenient for him to get to work downtown in the
damn morning. These four walls are supposed to be
the shelter from the storm. Four hundred damn years
and we're still shackled to a twisted tree –told to dance
like lil' sambos cause it'll please that blonde hair, blue
eyed Jesus as he pull our strings and gives a few of us,
flashy rings and Mercedes while the rest of us fight
"the American Dream!". But that's alright… that's
alright cause—Babylon is going to fall. Then you're
going to fall right along with it. *(He turns to leave.)*
Reverend, worst kind of nigger there is…don't even
know he's a damn nigger.

RAYMOND: Ty, that's enough. Damnit, that is your
brother.

TY: That nigger is no brother of mine.

RAYMOND: He is your brother.
He's your blood. You're the other half of the prophecy.
Rev. John McHenry Sr. is your father—and that's your
brother. the prophecy needs to be fulfilled. "Unite the
blood." Now more than ever you two need to come
together.
Been waiting a long time for you lions to roar-- as
brothers.
Ty…John, I should've told you! Held it inside so
long…waiting for your father to— But it's not too late.
Flesh look upon blood… Blood look upon flesh…love
each. Ty, all you have is each other.

(TY *picks up letter.*)

TY: Yeah, well, Cain killed Abel, now didn't he? (*He exits.*)

(*End scene*)

Scene Four:
The Angel Speaks

(*Next day*)

(RAYMOND *drags in the old Pastor's Chair.*)

(MCHENRY *enters with* ANGELA.)

(*She wears a red dress—suitcase in hand.*)

MCHENRY: I won't be too long, I promise. Just got to get some things and we'll go to the airport. Alright?

(RAYMOND *enters.*)

RAYMOND: Mrs McHenry, how you doing? She still not talking none?

MCHENRY: Been three days now. We're going back to Chicago. Hope that being around her parents might do some good.

RAYMOND: Might do the trick.

McHenry notices old chair is back.

MCHENRY: What happened to the new chair?

RAYMOND: Suppose someone broke in again. Guess they must've liked it.

(MAMA LOVE *enters.*)

MAMA LOVE: Reverend. Angela? Ray. You tell him?

RAYMOND: Boy, I hate to add more on your plate but we got to talk about some members of the congregation.

McHENRY: Not really my concern anymore.

RAYMOND: Well you know how we always have a get together afterwards for the Juneteenth Celebration— at Clarence and Sadie May Jenkin's House?

McHENRY: Inform them I'm going to be stepping down as the preacher of this church.

RAYMOND: Well you don't have to worry about addressing that particular issue with them.
Clarence didn't take the eviction notice too well and he kinda— burned their house down.

McHENRY: His house?

RAYMOND: Said he'd burn it to hell before he let some white devils kick him out. Sadie May and him both passed away from the fire, child is setting up funeral arrangements now.

McHENRY: Funeral arrangements?

RAYMOND: You know he built that home with his own hands. Don't think he could've lived with someone else tearing it down. Yeah, he decided to leave this earth with it.

McHENRY: That's impossible I just talked to her earlier today.

RAYMOND: Don't know how it happened last night.

McHENRY: Things can't get worse.

(WINTERS *enters*.)

WINTERS: Reverend McHenry.

McHENRY: Claire?

WINTERS: John, as a friend, I thought I should deliver this personally.

(WINTERS *hands document to* McHENRY.)

McHENRY: They're going to tear down the church?

RAYMOND: Not going to be happy till they tear this whole neighborhood down.

MCHENRY: I withdrew my name from the Minority Redevelopment Grant. How come members in the community still have eviction notices on their doors? And this?

WINTERS: The Fourth Ward Redevelopment Project is going thru. Once you stepped away from the project, Reverend Hopewell, was more than willing to sign on.

MCHENRY: Reverend Hopewell?

WINTERS: Yes. He told me he knew you. Funny how small the world is.

MCHENRY: He's white.

WINTERS: Yes, but he sees the potential for this place, and is greatly invested with a desire to pull the community up from their poverty.

MCHENRY: Pull up or push out?

WINTERS: I'm doing this for the sake of progress.

MCHENRY: The community center? This church? Those homes? Why?

WINTERS: It's nothing personal, John. If I didn't take advantage of the opportunity someone else would.

MCHENRY: What do you have to gain?

WINTERS: The future. This is where the future wants to be.

MCHENRY: But there is history here.

WINTERS: John, what is history but heirlooms, antiques and feeble hands trying to grasp a fragile past. Too scared to let go. Too scared to move forward. What is history except a pawn standing in the way of a king.

MCHENRY: (Reading document) I don't know how to fight this. I don't know what to do.

RAYMOND: Your father would—

MCHENRY: She's right. This was once a thriving—
A promise land for blacks. Now look at it. This
neighborhood looks like despair walked through and
placed his prints on every building he could touch.
Burnt out wrecks… Dilapidated structures… Shotgun
houses where beautiful homes once were. Black owned
stores replaced with—Fight—for this place?

RAYMOND: Blessed are the poor, Lord…Blessed are the
poor…

MCHENRY: I'm etched into the pillars—

RAYMOND: Then fight for that, Reverend. Fight for—

(MCHENRY *drops to his knees, his arms outstretched wide.*)

MCHENRY: Bless me Father, for I have— I know you
do things how you want, but I don't understand how
to make things right… Why you take my Angel's
voice? Why you got these people suffering? My wife,
nourishing, nurturing me…I neglected her, and I'm
sorry for that. Got so caught up in being bigger…
better than my father—I forgot to take care of this
community. God, I don't know how to fix this.
Searching for the words to pray but …

(Silence)

(Distant music/drums?)

ANGELA: The Lord is my shepherd…I shall not—

(Pause)

MCHENRY: I shall not want. *(Pause)* The Lord is my…

ANGELA: Lead them, John, they need you to lead them.

Mama Love steps out of the shadows.

MAMA LOVE: An Angel speaks…

McHenry rises to his feet…

MCHENRY: The Lord is my shepherd…

ANGELA: John…everybody listens to the preacher, nobody listens to the preacher's wife, but I want you to listen to me now.

MCHENRY: Angela.

ANGELA: Mama Love told me to make a cobbler and place what I value most into it. Then while it's still hot, take it and go see Old Lady Goody. I went , and before I could even speak to her, she spoke my name—Angela…Angel. She reached into the center of that cobbler, steam rising, then she grabbed my hand and—and when she let go, I opened my hand and saw my wedding ring.
I realized where I'm supposed to stand in this life. And baby, don't worry about legacy…

(ANGELA *places* MCHENRY'*s hand on her stomach.*)

MCHENRY: I'm going to be—?

ANGELA: I know where I stand now. Next to you. I don't know what you're supposed to do, but we're going to get through this together. Our fate, it's not the ragged wooden cross, or the one made of platinum, but it's inside you. It's your past, your present, it's your son. You got to stand for all of us—or else nobody will be around for a legacy.

MAMA LOVE: You startin' to understand the prophecy now?

RAYMOND: Roar mighty lion—roar.
I'll follow you to the frontlines of hell, Reverend.

MAMA LOVE: Let's hope we don't have to go that route.

RAYMOND: Just tell me what you want me to do, Reverend.

(TY *enters.*)

MCHENRY: I'm glad you came back.

TY: Somebody had to make sure you did something right for these people.

MCHENRY: I'm going to fix this—

(MCHENRY *moves towards* TY.)

(TY *pulls out a gun and points it at* MCHENRY.)

ANGELA: John!!!

TY: Don't –

RAYMOND: Put the gun away.

TY: Somebody got to stand for the community.

RAYMOND: Put that gun away, you don't want to do this.

MCHENRY: Ty—same blood. We can stand for the community together.

TY: All my life I stood alone… Wishing I had more… wishing I had somebody to call family…for a father—

MCHENRY: I can't make up for the past— but we can make a future.

RAYMOND: Listen to him, Ty.

TY: What future. We don't have no home?!!

(MCHENRY *chances it. Moves closer to* TY.)

MCHENRY: Grab a hold of me. Ty, all you got to do is come here— and we can win fight together.

McHenry stands arms outstretched g for Ty. McHenry embraces. The gun—to the ground. Brothers united.

MAMA LOVE: Blood United.

WINTERS: *(Claps)* United—but you will fall. So, Reverend, what will you tell your sheep, on Juneteenth? What will you tell them when that door is boarded up, padlocked—chained—waiting for bulldozer's to tear this church down! What will you do now?

McHENRY: I don't really know.

ANGELA: He's going to deliver the Juneteenth Sermon. That's what he's going to do.

WINTERS: I beg your pardon?

ANGELA: I didn't stutter.

MAMA LOVE: An Angel speaks!

McHENRY: Angela…?

ANGELA: Now, Ms Winters…it is *Ms* Winters isn't it? You asked *my husband* what *he* was going to tell *his* congregation. He's going to tell them what Juneteenth is all about. He's going to tell them about how my husband's father was a great minister. Just like his father before him. He's going to stand there at that pulpit and tell them that, all he can do is feed them with truth—and hope it fills them. Tell them about how two years after the emancipation proclamation, on June 19th, 1865—Juneteenth—the slaves in Texas were freed. Tell them how since that day—community, history, and legacy established this ward. It was that moment that we as a people decided we will never be chained again. You asked him what he's going to do. Well that man is going to preach!

(Lights shift.)

(McHENRY stands at the podium.)

McHENRY: Brothers and sisters, I'll be honest with you, I can't preach like my father and his father before him— but I can tell you a story. Would you like to hear a story? Now this story, might not be biblical –but clearly it's inspired by the Sacred Book. I'm going to tell you a story about this boy, five fishes, and two loaves of bread.

Now once upon a time, this little boy started climbing
that hill up to Jesus. Was willing to give the little bit he
had to help feed the many. Seeing the boy was willing
to give all he had to make a difference—others on that
hill, started to give the little bit that they had. And the
five fishes and two loaves began to grow. Grow into
ten fishes and fifty loaves of bread. And as he walked
up that hill, more people within that community felt
compassion to give, and to share, and they placed more
into that basket, and more into that basket—till the
basket was spilling over. By the time the boy reached
the hilltop—and presented the baskets of food—Jesus
smiled! And the feast that was given to the people.
Feed every last one—and was still leftovers.
Oh, church, I'm standing before you today to say—this
parable (miracle?) is us. This community! I'm standing
up here on this Juneteenth Morning and telling you
that once upon a time we depended upon ourselves
for this neighborhood to grow and thrive. Now, as
preacher of this church—you expect me to stand up
and roar like a lion. But the truth of the matter is—each
and every last one here is a lion. Not sheep like they
would like us to believe—but lions! It's time for all of
us who claim this neighborhood—to stand! To stand
and roar.

(RAYMOND *leads singing* None But The Righteous.)

McHENRY: And, when the city arrives with boards and
nails and chains to close this church down— hen that
Bulldozer rumbles—we're going to stand before them.
On this street—this Juneteenth Street. Hands clasped,
together, and hold fast. And to anyone that comes
to take what we have, we're going to say in a united
voice— "That this is *our home*! And it's *not* for sale. It's
not for sale!

(McHENRY *stands arms outstretched wide.*)

RAYMOND: Roar mighty lion roar!

MCHENRY: *(To congregation)* Roar! Roar! Mighty lions—
roar!

(Lights fade)

END OF PLAY

www.ingramcontent.com/pod-product-compliance
Lightning Source LLC
Chambersburg PA
CBHW070024110426
42741CB00034B/2458